Exploring
Suffolk by bus pass

Pip Wright

Pawprint Publishing
in collaboration with Suffolk Passenger Transport

ISBN 978-0-9548298-6-5
Published by **Pawprint Publishing**
14, Polstead Close, Stowmarket, Suffolk   IP14 2PJ

Other books by Pip Wright

Daniel Malden
Lydia
Death Recorded
I Read it in the Local Rag
(pub. by Poppyland Publishing)

Books by Pip & Joy Wright

The Amazing Story of John Heigham Steggall,
'The Suffolk Gipsy'
Newspapers in Suffolk (6 vols)
Grave Reports
Witches in and around Suffolk
Bygone Cotton

See all these at
www.pipwright.com

&

The Diary of a Poor Suffolk Woodman
(with Léonie Robinson, pub. by Poppyland Publishing)
See **www.poppyland.co.uk**

A list of my expeditions by bus

...Amounting to a little under two thousand miles, taking over eighty
hours and travelling on more than a hundred buses

Foreword

I have lived in East Anglia for very nearly twenty years now. I believe this would mean that I almost qualify for the title of being a genuine resident, if I hadn't moved from Norfolk to Suffolk, which probably makes me a foreigner in both counties.

During the whole of that time, I have been involved in either planning, driving or managing bus services, from the North Norfolk coast right across to Haverhill. I think I therefore have a fairly good knowledge of what is possible and take great delight in proving people wrong when they speak of bus travel as limiting or minimal. Even so, Pip Wright has greatly surprised and impressed me with the breadth, depth and variety of his excursions. A book like this could so easily become a bus enthusiast's diatribe; instead it is anything but!

Containing a wide variety of excursions, covering most of Suffolk, much of Norfolk and with helpful suggestions for the obligatory tea and cakes (plus the occasional pint), Pip opens up all sorts of possibilities and encourages readers to think for themselves as well. His observations of life 'on the buses' are intuitive and accurate, from the regular services to the once-a-week market-day bus, definitely a different animal and one I remember with fondness. Buses are about the people who ride them and Pip captures this well.

Suffolk is a wonderful county, and East Anglia a beautifully diverse part of the country. Most of us do not get out and about as much as we should and do not realise the possibilities that begin at the nearest bus stop. Here is a lovely way to get some exercise, see the countryside, meet people and relax in a suitable establishment all at the same time. What could be better?

Neville Jephcote: 'Senior Public Transport Development Officer'

suffolkonboard.com
suffolk passenger transport

At the time of going to print in May 2008, all information in this book was accurate, and all expeditions had been tried at least once. The author cannot be responsible for changes in routes and timetables that might come about after that. As has been discovered, not all changes are for the worse as alterations to routes in April 2008 have often shown.

This book makes little reference to using a bus-pass on Ipswich park-and-ride services, though this is an important function of the card and certainly not to be sneezed at.

Exploring
Suffolk by bus pass

In September 2007, I had a birthday. It was a big one.

My family staged a surprise party (and it **was** a surprise). People mouthed encouraging words like, "Don't forget to apply for your bus pass!"

So it was , the following Monday, clutching my birth-certificate as proof I was now a senior citizen, I went into the local Council Offices and had my photograph taken (badly).

"It will arrive within a month," I was told. It actually only took a week, and the very next day I embarked on my first voyage of adventure - to that outpost known as Bury St. Edmunds.

Now I must admit I have not been a regular user of buses during my junior years. I assumed that they were dirty, overcrowded and too infrequent to be worthy of my consideration. I grew up in a Suffolk village where buses came twice a week if you were lucky. How different it is today!

Admittedly it can take forever to get to places as you seem to pass through a sequence of villages known only to the most intrepid of explorers. But did you know that buses run from Ipswich to Aldeburgh and back every hour during the day? Would you believe that no fewer than nine buses a day ply between Stowmarket and Diss. Oh, by the way, your bus pass does allow you to cross international borders to places as exotic as Diss and Thetford, and they even allow you back without a passport.

No sooner had I taken charge of my bus-pass than a trip to Tourist Information furnished me with timetables to places I had only imagined in my wildest dreams - Burgate, Hemingstone, Dalham, Elmsett and Chelmondiston to name but a few. But whilst I may mock, and those at home watching me set out for pastures new might pass all manner of snide comments, it came as a complete surprise to me to discover what a delightful way this was of exploring Suffolk.

To begin with, I made for the towns, usually with a purpose, but as I began to discover other places and other purposes, my wish-list of places to travel to increased.

I have the advantage of living in the centre of Suffolk. Almost everywhere is reachable by lunchtime. My second trip to Saxmundham involved using two buses and I found, though I took a crossword with me, it was well into the return journey that I started it.

The first thing that strikes you is the panache with which drivers put these buses down lanes designed for bicycles, and find ways in and out of lines of parked cars as they negotiate housing estates. You also notice corners of the county you have never seen before, and are tempted to press the 'STOP' button and while away some time there until the next bus ambles through. All I can say is, 'why not?' That is what having a bus-pass is all about.

Expedition 1: From Stowmarket to Harwich
via Shotley (using the foot-ferry)
Bus 88A: Stowmarket to Ipswich: 27 minutes
Bus 97: Ipswich to Shotley: 32 minutes
Return: Bus 98: 42 minutes, Bus 88: 41 minutes

Buses can be erratic, though less than you might expect. On Saturdays, a number of those plying between Stowmarket and Ipswich are of the express variety and get you where you are going remarkably quickly. This one arrived early and zipped along the A14 in impressive style.

There is a sense of satisfaction as you streak into Ipswich, bus-laning past queues of stationary cars and into the centre of town. After a short wait, I boarded the first bus bound for Shotley. The 97 is more direct than the 98, but at the time of my trip, it did not run all the way down to the Marina (Some do now, following revision of the routes). Being a fine day, I knew I'd enjoy the amble along the waterfront from Shotley Gate. And you can always gather your strength in the Bristol Arms, only yards from the bus-stop.

Bus-drivers come in all shapes and sizes. This one was a bit of an entertainer. He warned us that if the bus became too full, we'd have to travel upstairs (it was a single-decker). As no more than six were travelling on that bus at any given time, his threat was not put to the test.

The walk from Shotley Gate to the Marina is a real pleasure. With the tide out, wading birds such as oyster-catchers and little-egrets could be seen searching for food in the estuary silt. As you make your way towards the marina, Harwich lies across the water to your right and the cranes and container-ships of Felixstowe fill the skyline straight ahead.

If you have time, there is the H.M.S. Ganges museum, free to all visitors. It is certainly worth a visit. And should hunger or thirst make an attack, the Shipwreck Inn offers good meals and a selection of ales. I was glad I had arrived in plenty of time.

Pictured above: the foot-ferry
Below left: the old light vessel
Below right: Harwich Maritime Museum

The foot-ferry only runs daily from the beginning of May until the end of September; with weekend crossings in April. All this is subject to weather conditions. The crossing to Harwich in 2008 costs just £1 each way for anyone with a bus-pass. But remember, the boat holds a maximum of 12 people, so in school-holiday times it can mean delays.

Our crossing was calm and enlivened by stopping at a former light vessel, anchored midstream, (pictured opposite) to pick up a passenger.

> **Alternative:** You have the choice to remain awhile at Harwich or stay aboard the ferry and continue on to Felixstowe dock.

I chose to get off at Harwich and I am glad I did. Everywhere you go in this town, it shouts its history. From the moment you step onto the old 'Halfpenny Pier,' signs draw you towards a host of heritage sites - the two lighthouses, both homes to museums, the treadwheel crane, the Electric Palace Cinema and the old Customs House to name but a few. I whiled away a happy hour in the Antiques Centre, housed in a magnificent old bank building, close to the former naval shipyard.

Robert Louis Stevenson said, 'To travel hopefully is a better thing than to arrive,' as though the anticipation would inevitably be better than what you might expect to find at the end of your journey. Not so! All I can say is if you've not explored Harwich, put it on your list of places to visit. You'll not be disappointed.

The ferry back to Shotley is designed to coincide with the arrival of a bus back to Ipswich. This being a 98, it ambled there through the attractive villages of Erwarton, with its fine church and hall, and Lower Holbrook with views across the Stour valley. It took longer but it was worth it.

Alternative: I was tempted to stop at Holbrook and to take to the footpath, but having neglected to bring a map, I pencilled it in as an idea for another day (see expedition 23)

The express bus back to Stowmarket appeared to go missing, so it was a 'round the houses' run home... a small blot on an otherwise terrific day.

Expedition 2: From Ipswich to Woodbridge via Bucklesham and back via Kesgrave.
Bus 179: 57 minutes   Return: Bus 65: 41 minutes

Getting into Ipswich was a bit of a trial. Parking and using my pass on the Park & Ride, I sat in front of someone in possession of a device that emitted what can only loosely be described as music. There was no escaping it.

Perhaps unwisely, I had left no margin for error as regards catching my intended bus from Ipswich Old Cattle Market. Fortunately we arrived just on time and I was able to hurriedly board the 179 for Woodbridge. The driver was surprised I should want to travel to Woodbridge that way as it takes a most circuitous route, but I assured him I was in no hurry.

It proved to be quite a scenic route by Suffolk standards, leaving Ipswich by the Bucklesham Road and heading out past the Suffolk Showground. We travelled in and around Kirton, then out and back on ourselves before joining quite the bumpiest and bendiest road to Newbourne. This was a point I could have chosen to stop and walk awhile. The Fox serves good food and vittles, and wildlife abounds in the area.

Alternative: It is not a bad idea to get the driver to drop you at the top of the lane leading to Hemley, where it is possible to walk down by one of the wilder parts of the River Deben. Alternatively, stay on the bus a while longer and get off at Waldringfield where the river walks are wonderful and, on occasions, boat-trips are available.

Arriving at Woodbridge in the knowledge that any one of a number of different routes would return me to Ipswich, I could amble without worrying about catching the next bus.

Woodbridge, by the tide-mill

Woodbridge, it seems to me, is a town dedicated to food and drink. There are delicatessens, wine-shops and eating-places of all colours. Also, it is a great place to shop - small independent shops thrive here as well as some of the more familiar High Street names.

Walking down by the river, there is the Tide-Mill to visit and any number of wading birds and boats to enjoy. Up in the town, a wander reveals all sorts of hidden corners. It is certainly a place to while away a few hours.

The 65 bus that I returned on starts from Rendlesham and runs at least a dozen times a day, meaning that some of the villages in that area (Such as Eyke and Melton) are particularly well served by public transport.

The return journey co-incided with several schools en-route finishing for the day, and for the first time I found myself on a fairly full bus. For the most part, rural buses are not well used and it is not unusual to find you are the only passenger on a forty-seater.

Expedition 3: From Combs Ford, Stowmarket to Hadleigh (with dog)
Bus 462: 40 minutes   Return: Bus 462: 38 minutes

I was interested to discover what the policy is regarding dogs on buses. I was told the decision lies with the driver, though well-behaved dogs should be accepted. Only if they are a nuisance or a danger are they likely to be refused. Charlotte, my seven year-old Cavalier King Charles spaniel accompanied me. The driver could not have been more welcoming. I learned that on this occasion, the same driver would be the one making the return run just over two hours after our arrival. Charlotte sat on my lap and seemed to enjoy the trip.

The route takes you cross-country through a number of villages. We passed the attractive church at Little Finborough, before circling around Wattisham base and off through Naughton and Whatfield. Naughton possesses one of the most charming of Suffolk pubs, the Wheelwright.

Alternatives: Between Whatfield and Hadleigh, the high ground gives you views of Kersey church on the opposite side of the valley. Leaving the bus at Whatfield you can find footpaths to Kersey (using O.S. Explorer map 196) where, on a Tuesday or Friday morning, you may catch a 772 back to Hadleigh. More intrepid walkers might continue on to Bower House Tye, where a 91 bus passes hourly to Hadleigh or Sudbury.

The thing that made this trip for me was discovering what was a real neighbourhood bus. The driver clearly knew everyone and took time to pass the time of day with them. I noticed one lady had brought him some of her garden produce. There was no talk of bus-stops here. In Whatfield in particular, we picked people up outside their houses. One lady, on disembarking at Hadleigh, was heard to say, "I'll probably be here later - if I'm not, don't wait for me." And I think he might well have done if she hadn't said that.

Hadleigh Guildhall

Hadleigh is a fine place to wander. The riverside walks, especially in Autumn, are lovely. My dog Charlotte thought so anyway. The churchyard is a gem, with the old Deanery Tower in one corner and the Guildhall in another. Around the town, the history of the place comes through in the names... Pykenham Way, Guthrum Road, Silk Mill Close... and the less convincing Tudor Chipshop. It's just a pity Hadleigh has so few seats on which to sit and ponder.

On our return, our driver managed to keep to the timetable, but still help the elderly with their purchases off the bus, and even have a moment or two's word with most of them. It was like a step back in time... the way we'd like to believe things used to be.

Expedition 4: From Stowmarket to Diss
Bus 456: 60 minutes   Return: Bus 458: 63 minutes

Nearly every Friday, there are auctions held at Gaze's saleyard at Diss. There is also an outdoor market. As a result extra bus-routes come into play. Daily, Diss is reached a number of times from Stowmarket, Bury St. Edmunds (route 304/338), Framlingham/ Stradbroke (route 118/482) and Ipswich (via Debenham or Mendlesham - route 113/114). On Fridays, you can go to Diss from Mendham (route 5), Wingfield (route 475) or from Worlingworth (route 4), passing through a number of the more isolated corners of Suffolk.

I went from Stowmarket along with a more elderly companion. The forty-seater buses lower to allow easy access when they stop, but smaller buses ply such routes as this. They have steps to negotiate, but our driver was used to helping those who had difficulty.

The journey we took there went by way of Bacton,

The mere at Diss

Eye and Mellis, and we arrived on time. The bus-station, such as it is in Diss, is close to decent-sized supermarkets (Morrison's and Tesco's). It is also just opposite the park and the famous mere, a lovely spot for a picnic on a summer's day. The town centre lies just around the mere. Diss has a small museum, a number of specialist shops and of course the auction rooms. I was aware that if I bought anything too huge, I'd have to come back another way to collect it. As it was, I came home empty-handed on this occasion, having enjoyed lunch at the auction rooms whilst for once, merely observing others making their purchases.

The return route took us through a slightly different cluster of villages including Burgate, Gislingham and Mendlesham, though it took almost the same time to do the journey as the trip there had.

By the way, we officially became what is known in the trade as 'twirlys' on this journey. In many counties (though not in Suffolk) the bus-pass is supposed to come into operation from 9:30 onwards, but occasions are bound to arise when you want to start your journey a few minutes before, which gives rise to the question, "Am I too early (twirly) to use my bus-pass?" Usually this seems to be perfectly OK, as it was in this instance.

Expedition 5: From Stowmarket to Needham -Market (with toddler in buggy)
Bus 87: 13 minutes   Return: Bus 87: 11 minutes

Most of the forty-seater buses have an area designed to allow for wheelchairs or unfolded child carriages. In reality, they are usually full of shopping trolleys. I was taking my grandchild on a bus for the first time, just down the road a short way to Needham Market. For two thirds of the year, Needham has a car-boot sale beside the lake on Wednesday and Saturday mornings. My grandson was much more keen to see the ducks and play on the swings and slides beside the lake. It is lovely place to take children, dogs or just yourself to walk and enjoy the wildlife. On this occasion, I even saw a kingfisher.

Alternative: If feeding animals is what you enjoy, you can always continue on the bus past Needham to Baylham where the Rare Breeds Centre lies about 200 metres from the bus-route. Or you could walk there from Needham along the Gipping Valley Path. Buses to Ipswich or to Needham & Stowmarket pass Baylham Mill Lane about twice an hour.

The fact that most of these buses lower to virtually pavement level makes it easier to bring push-chairs, wheel-chairs etc. aboard. On our return, there were fewer trolleys to compete with, so we weren't blocking the gangway to other passengers with our buggy.

Expedition 6: From Ipswich to Manningtree
(via Bentley)
Bus 96: 44 minutes   Return: Bus 96: 51 minutes

There is a route that runs about five times a day from Bildeston to Manningtree via Hadleigh (routes 730, 731), but having less time to spare, I took the quicker route from Ipswich instead. I had heard of the term 'driver's bus', meaning that some drivers regularly transported themselves and no-one else to places along the less popular routes. This must have been one of those. I had the bus to myself.

You can use this route to convey you to places worth visiting along the way. You pass right by the end of the lane to Jimmy's Farm, for instance. Also, the route goes through Tattingstone, crossing at one point, Alton Water.

Alternative: As this is a turnaround bus (the driver reaches the end of the route at Mistley, then drives the return route straight back) getting off at Tattingstone would give you well over an hour to explore the delights of the reservoir known as Alton Water before the same bus returns. Of course, you could always be more adventurous and walk by way of the track around the reservoir to Holbrook or Stutton, linking up with bus-route 92 or 98 to make your return to Ipswich - see expedition 23.

I stayed on the bus to Manningtree and remained there only briefly. (The bus continues to Mistley where it terminates and returns almost immediately) Though my visit was short, you could stay and return a couple of hours later. Walks along the river frontage are pleasant, though I prefer the marshes between Brantham and Manningtree Station. This is a particularly good place for bird-watching and an easy way to kill a couple of hours. (see expedition 28)

Alternative: You can even follow the River Stour path as far as Flatford Mill (of John Constable fame), walking up to East Bergholt and catching the 93 bus back to Ipswich or taking a 730 bus to Manningtree and returning by the 96 route.

Little Egret and Shelduck

Manningtree, you will discover, is full of naturalists and hikers, to whom it seems to appeal most.

Alternatives: If you take the bus all the way to Mistley, you can see the renowned Mistley Towers and even walk along the Essex Way up to the Heath where, in the derelict churchyard, Matthew Hopkins, the Witchfinder General is reputed to be buried. There is, of course, the opportunity to take a bus from Manningtree to the more attractive estuary port of Brightlingsea. From April 2008, it became possible to use one's bus-pass to explore other counties. As a result, this further trip is one that is strongly recommended.

Expedition 7: From Bury to Sudbury, then to Clare via Long Melford, and returning to Stowmarket

Bus 753 to Sudbury: 60 minutes
Bus 236 to Long Melford: 10 minutes
Bus 236 to Clare: 15 minutes/ to Sudbury: 25 minutes
Bus 111/461 to Stowmarket via Bildeston: 67 minutes

Bus Stations come in all shapes and sizes. Bury bus-station, like that at Mildenhall, is modern, spacious and, to use the contemporary jargon, 'fit for purpose.' Some places that claim to have bus-stations have in fact only depressing standing areas where you can catch buses. Sudbury and Diss fall into this latter group, and Ipswich rates little better. Norwich bus-station appears well-appointed, but struggles to accommodate the flow of buses that use it.

Growing in confidence regarding the use of buses and no longer so dependant on timetables, I set out from Bury St. Edmunds with no clear idea where I might end up. The route 753 from Bury to Colchester is an attractive one, passing through Lavenham, Long Melford & Bures, stopping at Sudbury. Most of the buses plying this route are double-deckers. It is amazing how different the world looks from

Lavenham

22

above. You can see the hidden places concealed behind high hedges, the walled gardens and views of the Suffolk countryside denied those stuck at ground level.

Lavenham is a place worthy of a stop, and with buses every hour, this is easily possible. On this occasion I continued on to Sudbury. A quick glance at timetables showed I could move on to Clare using route 236. Here I encountered a problem that regular bus users will be all too aware of - they had changed the timetable so that all the middle of the day buses only went as far as Glemsford. I decided, as I was to spend more time in Sudbury, I would use it to my advantage.

Sudbury is an odd mix. Parts are very old and very beautiful. Other parts are best forgotten. Also a lot of people visit Sudbury, most of them by car, so even crossing the road is a nightmare. But the town has its finer points too. Gainsborough's House is well worth a visit. There is a good collection of shops. Auctions are held here on alternate Thursday afternoons.

If you follow signs down to the Quay Theatre, you can take a range of superb walks along the River Stour and across the 'common lands.' From near Ballingdon Bridge, you can view the town and river from on high as you take the Valley Walk along the old railway track as far as the station.

I took my next bus to Long Melford, where every building that isn't already a gallery or antique shop probably soon will be. It is an enjoyable stroll down the main street (virtually the only street). There is also a good number of old and interesting pubs and inns serving food and drink.

Quay Theatre, Sudbury

This is a place where you could spend several days exploring. If you leave your bus at the northern end of the town (at the Bull or the Black Lion), you are close to three fine buildings. Long Melford Church is one of the grandest in Suffolk. As well as Melford Hall, there is the rather more lovely Kentwell Hall, but be warned - it is a good long step up the driveway.

At last, I caught my bus to Clare. This takes you through the attractive villages of Glemsford and Cavendish. Clare itself, though small, has much to offer.

The Abbot's House, Clare Priory

Every third Saturday morning, there is an auction. There is a splendid Antique Centre close to the old Priory and the Country Park, wherein you will find the Castle and the old Railway Station. There are circular walks - you can pick up free leaflets at the Park Centre - enabling you to take in the rich history and natural history of the area.

One of the finest buildings in Clare has to be the 'Ancient House', (shown here) now a museum, but open only in the Summer months. It can be found close to the  parish church, and displays some of the best examples of pargetting (decorated plaster-work) to be seen in Suffolk.

So far, this had proved a good day. I then encountered a problem I should have foreseen. I had miscalculated just how long it would take me to get home. I was meant to be back by about five. With all the will in the world, and taking the shortest route home possible, it would still take me in the region of three hours to catch three buses and return (late) to Stowmarket.

The route linking Sudbury, Stowmarket and Ipswich relies on meetings of buses in the old market square in Bildeston. Fair enough, three buses met, the system worked, but I was still late. It was my own fault for under-estimating the time it takes to travel by bus(es) and setting out with little more than a cursory glance at a timetable. And I didn't even take a mobile phone.

Expedition 8: From Ipswich to Orford and back
Bus 70A : Ipswich to Woodbridge: 39 minutes
Bus 71: Woodbridge to Orford: 43 minutes
The return might have been the same, but was not quite as expected

Orford on a cheerful sunny day is a great place to while away a few hours. I, by way of contrast, chose a wet autumn day, and even then that was not the end of my problems, as will become evident.

The 71 will take you all the way from Ipswich to Orford, but breaking the journey in two as I did is a much more attractive option.

> **Alternative:** Jumping off the bus at Rushmere, you could find your way across Rushmere Heath, then follow the Sandings Walk to Kesgrave, taking in the Mill Stream Nature Reserve, before returning on a 66 bus (they run about every 15 minutes).

The trip I had opted for is a tour for the person with all the time in the world. You pass through the attractive villages of Playford and Bealings (both Great and Small) before making for Woodbridge. Then aboard the 71, you continue past the entrance to Sutton Hoo, a place where you could easily choose to stop, provided you had any idea when there might be a return bus.

Across the heathlands of South-East Suffolk you then motor, as far as Hollesley.

> **Alternative:** On a finer day, you could disembark here and walk to Shingle Street, taking the coast path south to Alderton or Bawdsey. Buses (72/72A) run from both places back to civilisation - see expedition 13.

I however continued via Boyton and Butley all the way to

Orford.

Orford Castle

This is a place for the rambler, the naturalist and the historian. There is, in this tiny place, a fine castle, a lovely church and, down at the quay in the summer months you can get a ferry across to Orford Ness (now in the charge of the National Trust) or have a splendid meal combined with a boat-trip aboard the 'Lady Florence.'

There is an abundance of wonderful wildlife to enjoy by walking the riverside footpaths. In the village (surely you can hardly call Orford a town) you can find good food at the King's Head or sample smokehouse delights at the Orford and Butley Oysterage. You can also visit the underwater exhibition above the craft shop where you can learn about the shrinking Suffolk coastline and view artefacts discovered in dives off Dunwich.

Alternative: I have discovered that if you leave the bus close to the old Butley priory, you can follow the Suffolk Coast Path down to Butley River where, in the summer, by arrangement with Butley Pottery (phone: 01394 450843), you can get a ferry across and complete the journey to Orford on foot.

When the time came to return, the bus arrived punctually, but it was clear to the three passengers that boarded her that all was not well. We made it as far as the Butley Oyster pub before she gave up the ghost and refused to be our bus any more.

One of our party disappeared into the pub in anticipation of a replacement appearing sometime or other. In the end, we weren't that late, as any attempt to cover the normal devious route was abandoned and we were taken directly by sprinter bus back to our separate destinations in Woodbridge and Ipswich.

Oh, and by the way, if you chose that day to visit Sutton Hoo or Shingle Street believing a bus would arrive to carry you home, I hope you didn't get too wet waiting a further two hours for the next one.

Expedition 9: From Brandon to Thetford, then to Bury by way of Mildenhall
Bus 40: to Thetford: 15 minutes
Bus 201: to Mildenhall: 55 minutes
Bus 356: to Bury: 37 minutes

A friend was working in Brandon, so this was an opportunity to begin my journey somewhere different. I hitched a lift and found myself in Brandon at nine in the morning. People had spoken disparagingly of Brandon as 'bandit country' and the like, but it does have its saving graces. Firstly it has the River Ouse. You can hire rowing boats at the Bridge House, or take a walk along the river to Santon Downham, where you have no fear of being stranded.   Buses pass Santon Downham Church about once an hour bound for either Thetford or Mildenhall (route 200/201) or Bury (route 333).   This is one of the loveliest parts of East Anglia, and an area rich in wildlife.

Whilst in Brandon, you can also sample the beer at Brandon's own micro-brewery.   Try a taste of 'Rusty Bucket' or 'Norfolk Poacher' before continuing on your way. The problem of catching buses in Brandon is finding the bus-stops: even rarer are timetable boards. I flagged down a Thetford bus and fortunately it stopped. It was a route 40 bus which runs about four times a day between Kings Lynn and Thetford. It carried me quite directly from Brandon to Thetford, where the bus-station is pleasantly situated beside the river.

Close to the bus-station at Thetford

There is much to recommend Thetford, though its faults are many. Its medieval heart has gone, but there are reminders everywhere of its historic past.

Signs like 'Minstergate' sit uneasily beside 'Service Area Riverside West.' On foot, you can discover the Cluniac Priory remains, the massive castle mound, the old Gaol House, the Ancient House Museum, the Nuns' Bridges and the Charles Burrell Traction Engine Museum. Exploring Thetford can easily fill a day, and more besides.

The route 201 to Mildenhall, as mentioned before takes you by way of Santon Downham, a true forest gem of a place, and Wangford Warren, where keen aircraft spotters may take time out to visit the viewing area for Lakenheath air base. The landscape of this part of Suffolk is a strange mix of heathland and fen. You pass Eriswell Hall Barns, home to regular auctions.

Mildenhall has a fine bus-station, though I saw little of the town as my bus for Bury left almost at once. On the 356 bus, you pass along lightly wooded roads beset by grey squirrells. This route alternates hourly with the 355, which serves a different set of villages, offering another terrific opportunity for a splendid stroll.

Alternative: My bus passed through the attractive village of Tuddenham St. Mary. If you alight there and follow the footpath behind the village green and across Cavenham Heath, you eventually arrive at Icklingham, where a 355 will carry you to Bury or back to Mildenhall. (Described in detail in expedition 11)
The Icklingham area is full of good walks. You can take in West Stow Saxon Village and pick up the 333 service at West Stow Church, which links Bury and Thetford three times a day in each direction.

I notice from my notes that I made mention of the fact the four buses I used that day (including one more back to Stowmarket) all arrived on time and took pretty much the designated time to complete their journeys. By the time I had finished this book I was expecting, on most of my expeditions, this to be the case.

A quiet corner at Thetford Priory

Dalham

Expedition 10: From Bury to Newmarket and back
Bus 311: to Newmarket:
      48 minutes
Bus 11: to Bury: 30 minutes
Bus 386 to Onehouse:
      50 minutes

Accompanied by my mother I set out for Newmarket, home of the sport of Kings. The 311 route takes in a number of villages and there are things to look out for. Little Saxham church with its round tower is one of the first landmarks to spot. After that, the bus ambles via Barrow and Ousden to Dalham. Look out for the old windmill and a village full of thatched houses. We were able to appreciate the autumn colours as the road rose through the woods and parkland of Dalham Hall. It had rained heavily the night before, and streams were full.

Moulton Bridge on a day when the river was less full

This became even more evident as we came into Moulton. Our road ran through a ford, normally just a trickle that is the River Kennett. On this occasion, lower vehicles would not have made it. Our bus splashed through beside the old packhorse bridge that has become the symbol of the village of Moulton.

We approached Newmarket in the best way possible, coming down Warren Hill with the sun shining and a fair number of racehorses out on the gallops.

On the gallops at Newmarket

The bus station in Newmarket is conveniently postioned at one end of a covered mall that leads to the main street. It is easy and relaxing to take time out. If you are after food and refreshment, you should consider the restaurant at the Museum of Horseracing, where the food is good and cheap. If it is fine, you can enjoy eating in a comfortable courtyard. The museum too is well worth a look.

Alternatives: Had we had more time, Newmarket is a good place to travel from to other places. There are buses to Ely every hour and to Cambridge half-hourly. Four buses a day travel to and from Haverhill.

Our return journey was meant to be quicker. The 11 route starts at Cambridge and uses more main roads than the bus we had arrived on. However, as someone had chosen to transport a boat approaching the size of the QE2 down the road ahead of us, our return was unavoidably delayed.

So far, little has been said in praise of time spent in the town of Bury St. Edmunds. We went on Wednesday, which is market day, and there is an extensive market. Bury is a splendid place to shop, and it seems you can stop and grab a coffee almost anywhere, be it the library, the book-shop or one of a host of pavement cafés.

The Abbey Gardens are well worth a visit at any time of year, and within the old abbey walls, is Suffolk's only cathedral, (see right) complete with newly-built tower. Nearby, and just opposite the recently renovated Theatre Royal, you will find the Greene-King museum of brewing. Moyses Hall Museum is right in the centre of town. You will find simply ambling down the ancient streets of Bury is a delight.

At the front of the Abbey ruins in Bury

Alternatives: These are just a few of the pleasures of Bury. And of course, you can always use it as a place from which you can catch another bus to... the Henry Watson pottery at Wattisfield (service 304 - see expedition 29), visit Ickworth House at Horringer (service 344/345), or the Lackford Lakes nature reserve (service 355) - all just a short bus ride away.

Expedition 11: From Mildenhall to Bury allowing time for a walk across Cavenham Heath.
Bus 355: Mildenhall to Icklingham: 13 minutes
Bus 356: Tuddenham to Bury: 22 minutes

You can work this from either Bury or Mildenhall and walking from either end of the walk. I chose to catch the 355 at Mildenhall. It was a clear and crispy autumn morning and I left the bus at the Red Lion at Icklingham. Walking back in the direction I had come, I found a lane which leaves the main road at an angle close to the community centre. This soon fades into a track which reaches the river at a bridge, now closed even to walkers. It seems only a short while since cars were permitted to use this bridge. However, downstream about 50 metres, there is a new footbridge, enabling you to enter the Cavenham Heath nature reserve. Parts of this are closed during the nesting season where the reserve is home to a wide range of rare birds such as the nightjar and stone-curlew. Unusual plants and other forms of wildlife are also to be found.

> **Alternative:** Instead of crossing the heath, you could stay beside the River Lark and follow the Lark Valley Path all the way past Barton Mills and into Mildenhall. Plenty of buses run from there to Bury, Thetford and other places.

The track cuts across the heath in a straight line. It forms part of the old Roman road, the Icknield Way. Being on the Breckland, even after heavy rain, it is not particularly muddy and it is easy going, even if you take one of the paths across the heath. There are also wooded areas to enjoy. The winter wildlife I found included woodpeckers, flocks of fieldfares and several interesting fungi.

I had over two hours before I could expect to catch my bus to Bury, so there was no need to hurry. It is a couple of miles of easy walking. It is something to savour, especially on a day such as this.

On Cavenham Heath

Eventually, you find you are back on tarmac road. Gradually, you come into Tuddenham, passing horses, sheep, cattle and turkeys. Then there is the village pond and at the front of the green there is a bus-stop. Here, I was able to catch the 356 back to Bury.

Expedition 12: From Brandon to Kings Lynn, returning at length to Stowmarket

Bus 40: Brandon to King's Lynn: 1 hour 18 minutes
Bus 40: King's Lynn to Brandon: 1 hour 8 minutes,
then on to Thetford: 13 minutes
Bus 333: Thetford to Bury: 55 minutes
Bus 386: Bury to Stowmarket: 55 minutes

Though this book is essentially about exploring Suffolk, I was keen to see how far I could travel under the pre-April 2008 bus-pass regulations. Before then, one could only use a bus-pass to visit towns and villages in adjacent counties so as long as you began or ended any journey you chose to make in the county that issued your pass.

Alternatives: In this way, I found I could go from Bury to Cambridge (route 11), Haverhill to Cambridge (13), Lowestoft to Norwich and beyond (X2), Lowestoft to Great Yarmouth (1), Framlingham to Harleston and Norwich (569), from Bury via Sudbury to Colchester (753), Newmarket to Soham & Ely (12) and a number of other such possible excursions.

The bus from Brandon to King's Lynn was the first full bus I had encountered. It was a Saturday and this is obviously a popular route. It was also a grander bus than usually operates such services - reclining seats, foot-rests; even a toilet.

The journey takes you past the 'giant golf-balls' on the M.O.D. base at Feltwell and on across the flat lands that form the edge of fenland Norfolk.

Once there, I had about two and a half hours before I intended to return. King's Lynn is a town justly proud of its heritage. Yet this is not what greets you as you step away from the bus-station. To begin with, you are surrounded by modern shops. Readers of this book may sense the way I seem to be drawn towards water, and sure enough, I soon found myself beside the old Customs House on the quay. There is so much to admire and enjoy about the ancient town of Lynn. There are the magnificently restored houses and a cluster of museums reflecting Lynn's maritime past.

Lynn Customs House

Town Hall and Gaol buildings

As you wander between the market places, you come to understand that this is a very cosmopolitan place; a variety of different languages being spoken in the street. Then you realise this is the way it always was, with sailors from many different lands frequenting the town and the riverside areas.

Corners of Lynn, beside the river

King's Lynn is home to a handful of festivals celebrating music, theatre, literature and art & craft. It warrants far more than the couple of hours I had permitted myself on this occasion.

I was returning the way I had come, though those a little more adventurous than myself might work out a return via Lowestoft. My journey home was remarkably easy and efficient time-wise. I have mentioned before the difficulty of finding the right bus-stops in Brandon (the timetables refer to shops that no longer exist and roads that aren't marked on the map inside the timetable), so it was simpler to run on through to Thetford. Under the old bus pass arrangements as this meant going from Norfolk to Norfolk, the driver agreed it was to be regarded as two journeys - from Lynn to Brandon, then from Brandon to Theford.

My bus to Bury (service 333) left soon after I arrived in Theford and the Stowmarket bus linked with it perfectly. Connections don't always work this well, but from a nine o'clock start at Brandon, I'd been to Lynn, spent over two hours there and arrived back in Stowmarket soon after five.

Expedition 13: Martlesham to Bawdsey & back
Bus 63: Martlesham to Woodbridge: 10 minutes
Bus 72: Woodbridge to Bawdsey Ferry: 29 minutes
Then, either: **Ferry across to Felixstowe Ferry and**
Bus 173 to Martlesham: 44 min.
or: **Bus 72A: Alderton to Woodbridge: 21 minutes &**
Bus 165: Woodbridge to Martlesham: 6 mins.

Martlesham Water Bridge is a good point to begin a circular route. You can park nearby and there are plenty of buses that stop there.

I woke up on a fine bright autumn day and fancied an expedition I'd not yet tried. The 72 service to Bawdsey Ferry from Woodbridge cuts across Sutton Heath and makes for Hollesley. When I enjoyed this trip in the winter, the route took you close to the Penal Colony and you were able to enjoy views of the horses in the charge of the Suffolk Punch Trust. Now the route is a little more direct, passing through Alderton and Bawdsey village before reaching the point where the River Deben enters the North Sea.

Looking across to Felixstowe Ferry

Alternatives: During the summer months, or at weekends in the winter, you can take a small boat across to Felixstowe Ferry where you can find an assortment of eating-places and maybe even take some fresh fish home for tea.

The 173 service then returns you to where you began, though you may prefer to remain awhile in Felixstowe before finding a later bus back.

When I first tried this in late October, I was left with a pleasant alternative. Walking around the point at Bawdsey, and in front of Bawdsey Manor it is possible to follow the Suffolk Coast Path along Bawdsey Beach until the footpath returns you to the village. (It is always handy on occasions like this to have a map of the area with you - in this case, O.S. Explorer map 197) Then, following the road to Alderton, you happen upon the oasis that is the Swan public house, conveniently situated beside a bus-stop.

From there, suitably refreshed, I was able to take a route 72A bus to Woodbridge, followed by a 165 bus back to Martlesham. On a Saturday in April, I repeated this trip, but this time making the crossing and returning on a 173.

Expedition 14: From Laxfield to Beccles and back
Bus 532: Laxfield to Beccles: 1 hour 12 minutes
Bus 521: Beccles to Halesworth: 36 minutes
Bus 532: Halesworth to Laxfield: 23 minutes

A bus runs five days a week from Laxfield to Beccles. On two of those days, you can go on to Lowestoft. We went on a day when Beccles was the full extent of the journey. This was another of those social gatherings on board. Clearly the same people travel this route on a regular basis and all know one another as well as the driver. People wandered around offering sweets and we were made to feel very welcome.

The part of the journey to Halesworth is fairly quick and passes the magnificent splendour that is Heveningham Hall. Once beyond Halesworth, the route becomes more unpredictable, as if searching every lane and byway in that part of Suffolk. You pass St.Peter's Brewery and a number of fine old churches before finally arriving in Beccles.

St. Peter's Brewery

We all got off by the New Market Place, but it is worth noting that departures from Beccles are more reliably worked from the Old Market Place at the lower part of town (At the time of printing, being reconstructed).

Beccles is a pleasant town at the edge of the Broads. You can take boat-trips, visit the church or museum or just enjoy the shopping. There are plenty of good eating places, some offering river views. If I put on weight, I attach the blame to Twyfords' Belgian chocolate cheesecake. Such things are hard to say no to.

On the river at Beccles

We might have remained in Beccles until the return bus appeared, but it was easy to split the return journey into two parts. This time, the 521 bus took a more direct line to Halesworth. This gave us just about an hour to explore Halesworth, hardly time enough; but having gathered more timetables, it became clear that we would be able to travel this end of Suffolk by way of a number of other routes. The return to Laxfield was relaxed, as had been the whole day.

Expedition 15: Martlesham Heath to Felixstowe and back by a circuitous route
Bus 173: From Martlesham Heath to Felixstowe: 32 minutes
Bus 163: From Felixstowe to Ipswich: 41 minutes
Bus 66: From Ipswich to Martlesham Heath: 30 minutes

Tesco's at Martlesham Heath is another good place to begin a circular route. You can park nearby, plenty of buses stop there, and you can always buy your supper and take it home with you afterwards. The 173 service from there takes a fairly scenic route to Felixstowe, by way of Brightwell and Kirton. This was a smaller bus, more appropriate for some of the lanes involved. I disembarked at Great Eastern Square. This bus continues down to Old Felixstowe and Felixstowe Ferry, mentioned before with regard to my Bawdsey trip (expedition 13).

> **Alternative:** Felixstowe, these days, extends a long way down this section of coast and it is possible to take buses either to the docks at the mouth of the Orwell where a foot-ferry can be found to enable you to cross to Harwich, or down to the front if you don't feel like walking the half-mile or so to the sea.

The promenade stretches some distance and can be enjoyed at any time of year as long as you are well protected against the easterly winds that tend to drive in off the North Sea. You can get coffee and lunch at various places from the Spa Pavilion to all points south.

I quite like Felixstowe, especially out of season. Any place that boasts two good antiquarian bookshops is all right by me.

My visit this time was brief and just an hour after arriving, I was boarding another bus to Ipswich. I chose the 163 as it takes you via Levington and Nacton, close to the Orwell foreshore.

Alternative: A good idea for a walking day is to time it so you arrive at Nacton, walk the couple of miles downriver beside the Orwell to Levington. Then take lunch at the Ship before continuing on past the Marina to Trimley where you can catch the bus back.

On this occasion I stayed on my bus as it trundled along beside autumnal grounds belonging to Amberfield School. We came into Ipswich around the docks. At the time of writing, this is a huge redevelopment area and will doubtless eventually become the star in Ipswich's crown.

Close to Ipswich Docks,
January 2008

As things stand, the ancient churches of St. Peter & St. Mary at the Quay and Wolsey's Gate look most precarious amongst the demolition and rising buildings. It's worth a wander through the docks at any time, and right now it's rather like returning to see the changes in a garden brought about by the different seasons. You want to come back every so often to see what is different from the last time. Most Ipswich buses end their journeys near the docks and you can easily take time out by strolling through the back of the bus-station.

Ipswich is worth a mention at this point. though it clearly has its faults as a town, there are many things to recommend it. Christchurch Mansion is a gem and it is FREE!

You can also enjoy the Ipswich Museum in High Street (pictured here), try the Transport Museum or go for a swim at Crown Pools. These are just a few of a host of attractions on offer, from river trips to guided tours to dry-skiing.

The bus I took back from Ipswich to Martlesham Heath was the 66, an amazing service that runs every 15 minutes during the day and once practically every hour during the night. The route to Martlesham Heath takes in the warren of roads that make up Kesgrave and Grange

Farm, including an odd section of 'guided track' designed to enable buses to cut though from Kesgrave to Martlesham. High kerbs channel the bus wheels, so for a short section they operate almost like trams.

Then it was back to where I had started. Being short of time, I had taken just three hours to complete my journey.

Expedition 16: A circular tour from Framlingham to Snape Maltings and back again
Bus 63: Framlingham to Melton: 28 minutes
Bus 165: Melton to Snape: 25 minutes
Bus 195: Snape to Saxmundham: 11 minutes
Bus 197: Saxmundham to Framlingham: 47 minutes

Bus journeys may serve as a means of getting from one place to another. Alternatively, they can become a significant part of a day out. During the winter, I took my mother with me on a rather longer trip than this to prove that such an excursion isn't really as exhausting as it sounds and well within the capability of those a little more elderly than myself. We had travelled, on that occasion, from Stowmarket to Eye, then to Framlingham and Snape before finding a different route back. With altered timetables, that expedition is no longer as easy, so I've shortened this trip and added the last expedition in this book.

These tours offer the chance to visit and enjoy some of the smaller places that can nevertheless boast a good regular bus service.

There is something charming about Framlingham. It appears to attract interest without being overrun most of the time. The castle is well worth a visit. The mere that lies between castle and college attracts a wide variety of wildlife. Herons in particular were plentiful the day we were there. We took a coffee break at the Crown, an inn of some antiquity and a cosy, welcoming atmosphere. Comfortable seats, friendly waitresses and toasted tea-cakes always go down well, to my way of thinking.

Looking across to Framlingham Castle

Most buses entering or leaving Framingham use Bridge Street, which makes life easy for travellers such as ourselves. The service 63 runs through a number of small villages on its way to Wickham Market, Woodbridge and Ipswich.

Rather than go as far as Woodbridge to change buses, I disembarked at Melton Chapel, knowing the 165 would be along soon. It is worth doing this if the connection looks like being a bit tight. You then enjoy a pleasant run through

Blaxhall, Tunstall and Rendlesham. At one point, you pass the old gateway to Campsey Ash Abbey as it looks across at the barbed wire surrounding the former U.S. airbase of Bentwaters.

Snape Maltings is a good target for a visit. There is so much to do and see. There are short boat-trips at certain times (often as short as 45 minutes, so they can fit between bus times). The Snape Maltings website gives you further details. There is a host of shops as well as a tea-room, pub and restaurant.

At Snape Maltings

Alternatives: There are picturesque walks beside the River Alde, and should you wish, you could catch a 165 bus to Aldeburgh, confident that the 64 service runs hourly from there back to Ipswich.

We might have remained on the bus to Aldeburgh or Thorpeness, but we left the pleasures of the coast for another day, and after spending a couple of hours at Snape, we began to head back.

There is a choice regarding the return. I opted for the occasional 195 mini-bus which runs to Saxmundham, followed by the 197, a school route that takes on passengers and runs back to Framlingham. Clearly, we could have returned the way we had come earlier, or even remained aboard the 165 from Snape to Ipswich from where the 118 goes by way of Witnesham, Otley and Cretingham back to Framlingham. The 119 also operates all day between Saxmundham and Framlingham

Alternative: It is worth noting that it is at least as easy to do this trip the reverse way round.

Expedition 17: From Diss to Bungay and back again
Bus 580: Diss to Bungay: 40 minutes
Bus 580: Bungay to Diss: 40 minutes

A large number of routes covering Suffolk and the Norfolk border run east-west and this was no exception. The 580 service enables travel almost hourly between Diss and Great Yarmouth, stopping at Harleston, Bungay, and Beccles. I chose to try this route as far as Bungay. A few years ago, driving from Diss to Bungay would have meant passing through all the Waveney valley villages such as Brockdish, Needham, Redenhall and Wortwell. This bus takes you along that route, and a very pleasant run it is.

Bungay as a town has much to recommend it. There is quite an assortment of antique shops, a castle and a small museum. In the centre of the town is St. Mary's church, now redundant, but well worth a visit.

In the churchyard are the remains of the former nunnery (pictured above).

Alternative: A trip to Tourist Information Centre or library will furnish you with excellent leaflets on the Bungay Town Trail and describing a number of walks around the town.

Should you choose to travel further along this route, you can take time out at Fritton Lake or St. Olaves, exploring the Haddiscoe marshes and the old priory remains (for more details, see expedition 34).

As I said, according to the timetable, buses should arrive hourly throughout most of six days a week. The bus I had intended to return by did not arrive at all, so after a cold hour in a bus-shelter, I finally boarded another bus to return to Diss. This was the first and only time during the writing of this book that a bus I had planned to catch failed to materialise.

Expedition 18: A long circular tour starting and
finishing at Framlingham (Wednesdays only)
Bus 569: Framlingham to Harleston: 40 minutes
Bus 580: Harleston to Beccles: 48 minutes
Bus 534: Beccles to Southwold: 47 minutes
Bus 601: Southwold to Halesworth: 28 minutes
Bus 521: Halesworth to Saxmundham: 26 minutes
Bus 63: Saxmundham to Aldeburgh: 29 minutes
Bus 165: Aldeburgh to Woodbridge: 47 minutes
Bus 63: Woodbridge to Framlingham: 40 minutes

This was a bit of an endurance test and is not really
recommended in its entirety as a project for just one day. I
was keen to see how far it was possible to travel in a single
working day. In the end, it all worked remarkably well and
I covered nearly 200 miles in under nine hours. As some of
the connections were quite tight, I planned alternatives
should one bus turn up late. I should point out that this is
one of four routes I had to redesign in the light of changes to
the bus services in April 2008. Some months earlier, I had
travelled at least as far as this, starting and finishing at
Aldeburgh and circling in the opposite direction.

Beginning at Framlingham, just after nine in the
morning every Wednesday, the 569 route runs to Norwich
by way of Harleston, returning in the afternoon. It solves
the problem of going north. Most bus routes in Suffolk
travel east-west. This, at least was one that went the other
way, so I used this route to travel as far as Harleston. It is
easy to become blasé about the Suffolk countryside when
you are surrounded by it, but this start to my journey
showed Suffolk at its very best on a bright spring morning.

I had a quick wander about the small town of Harleston, an interesting place of small independent shops, before returning in good time to the bus-stop.

Note: It is worth noting that regular routes adhere quite rigidly to timetables. If a driver finds he is ahead of time, he will usually stop and wait until he is right. But with once-a-week buses, no such adherence to published times can be relied upon. They do have a habit of turning up early.

The 580 passed through Bungay (see expedition 17) then took the low-ground route through Geldeston and Gillingham as it approached Beccles.

Alternative: Here you can easily jump off your bus and wander down to Geldeston Lock where there is a pub more easily reached on foot (or by boat) than by car. Remember, buses run this route almost hourly. By arrangement, you can take the ferry that returns you to Beccles. (see www.bigdogferry.co.uk)

I had only allowed for a short break in Beccles - long enough for a coffee, before finding myself bound for Southwold on a 534 bus.

Southwold

Southwold is a splendid place to explore. Even if the sea seems less than inviting (it was November when I first made this trip), the pier has some unusual attractions, the shops, galleries and eating places have a charm all their own. Or you could wander down to the harbour, returning across the marshes. In Summer, you could take the ferry across to Walberswick.

I had allowed myself about thirty minutes; as long as I was to spend anywhere on a hectic day. My bus (601) to Halesworth arrived. Along the way, again I passed places that might have happily occupied me for a good part of any other day.

> **Alternative:** Several of these places are worth a visit themselves, but Blythburgh for the keen walker and naturalist is a treat to savour. The tidal marshes attract all manner of wildlife and you could easily take a day out here, returning by bus(es) later.

The recently amended 521 route is another of those useful north-south links that now joins Leiston, Saxmundham, Halesworth and Beccles almost every hour throughout the day. It is quick and efficient, and linked me with my next bus from Saxmundham to Aldeburgh.

From there, just two further buses would return me to Framlingham.

Aldeburgh

Expedition 19: Bury - Haverhill - Newmarket - Bury
Bus 345: Bury to Haverhill: 53 minutes
Bus 225: Haverhill to Newmarket: 49 minutes
Bus 11: Newmarket to Bury: 30 minutes

This excursion can be undertaken either way round. As the buses to Newmarket and Haverhill were scheduled to leave Bury at the same time, I chose the one that arrived first. The route from Bury to Haverhill (service 345) is a pleasant one, running in and out of attractive villages like Horringer, Chediston and Barnardiston. Unfortunately, the coach was grubby and covered in litter and graffitti; added to which the only person able to see through any of the mud-splattered windows was the driver. For all that, we made good progress and, as has usually proved the case in my travels, arrived at the designated time.

Haverhill is not a place that endears itself to me. However, it has a fine Town-Hall Arts Centre where you can find clean toilets and a good cup of coffee. It is also a place from which you can catch buses to Cambridge every half-hour and several times a day to Saffron Walden or Sudbury.

The bus-station is a dispriting place with very little guidance as to where or when you might catch a bus. Those timetables displayed are out of date and unreliable. Fortunately I carried mine with me.

Haverhill Town Hall (left) and a regular visitor to the bus-station (above)

The trip from Haverhill to Newmarket is a delight. I am not exaggerrating when I say I saw a sparrowhawk, a fox and a kingfisher from inside the bus (route 225) during this short run which passes through the lovely villages of Gt. Wratting, the Thurlows and Dalham. At Lidgate (pictured here) you can see the church perched imposingly above the village, as if to remind you of the castle that once stood above it on the hill.

Alternative: You could leave the bus here and take to shanks' pony, exploring the old motte & bailey before following tracks to Wickhambrook, (using O.S. Explorer map 210) where buses (service 344) can be found to return you to Bury or to Haverhill.

Lidgate

The final leg of the journey was quick. The Cambridge to Bury (route 11), as I had already discovered, is one of the fastest and most efficient ways of travelling across the county. It took the bus-driver little longer than it would have taken me to drive that distance in my car.

Expedition 20: Stowmarket to Lavenham via Bury & Sudbury and back
Bus 386: Stowmarket to Bury: 57 minutes
Bus 370: Bury to Sudbury: 47 minutes
Bus 753: Sudbury to Lavenham: 30 minutes
Walk to Monk's Eleigh
Bus 111: Monk's Eleigh to Bildeston: 6 minutes
Bus 461: Bildeston to Stowmarket: 29 minutes

Of the two routes linking Stowmarket and Bury St. Edmunds, I prefer the 386. It is slightly quicker and passes through more pleasant countryside.

As regards Bury to Sudbury, I had not used the 370 route before, so I tried it on this occasion. I could have gone straight to Lavenham on the 753 from Bury, but I am glad I took this roundabout route. The road through Whepstead and Hartest is pleasant, and I arrived at Sudbury having finished most of my crossword and having enjoyed a thoroughly pleasing cross-country amble by bus.

The 753 route tends to use a double-decker, as I had earlier discovered, and the best view is from up top. Leaving Sudbury, you quickly find yourself passing through Long Melford and out towards Acton. You get great views of the llama farm: after that it is only minutes before you reach Lavenham.

I had allowed myself three hours to enjoy the galleries and shops of Lavenham and to undertake the walk to Monk's Eleigh. If you haven't visited the church, the Guildhall and wandered around Lavenham's wonderful buildings before, then allow far longer. This was winter and though not everywhere was open, at least there were fewer tourists around.

For a tourist 'honeypot' Lavenham is quite poorly served by buses. The 753 route alone, from Bury to Sudbury (and on to Colchester) provides just a bus an hour in each direction.

There are several ways you can walk from Lavenham to link up with another service. Using O.S. Explorer map 196, I found tracks referred to as Clay Lane and Nova Scotia Lane. These were not simply footpaths, but more akin to old Green Lanes, firm underfoot (this was late November), with trees growing either side and overhead, so much of it was like walking down a tree-clad tunnel.

Clay Lane, leaving Lavenham

This walk, a little less than four miles is truly wonderful. The only sounds you hear are those made by woodpeckers and pheasants. You share the countryside with squirrels and deer. When I reached the end of Clay Lane, I could see as many as five church towers; yet these still did not include the very one I was heading for - that of Monk's Eleigh.

I arrived at Monk's Eleigh in time for a cup of coffee and piece of (heavenly) cake at Bridge Farm Barns (Corncraft), before flagging down a III bus to Bildeston. As I'd found before, this links well with the Stowmarket (461) bus and before I knew it, I was back.

Expedition 21: Debenham to Ipswich and back
Bus 114: Debenham to Ipswich: 39minutes
Bus 116: Ipswich to Debenham: 55 minutes

There are several Suffolk bus-routes where pairs of services alternate. The Mildenhall - Bury buses (355, 356) and the Stowmarket - Diss buses (456, 458) come into this category. In a similar way, you can travel to Ipswich from Debenham taking one of two or more routes. The 114, which begins its journey at Diss, is the faster way, travelling along the A140 and beside Shrubland Park to Claydon before joining the A14 and entering Ipswich. It is worth noting that this bus heads for the rail-station, not the bus-station, so it may be best to disembark at Museum Street.

I have already briefly mentioned a few of the more pleasurable attractions of Ipswich. On this occasion, it was less than a month before Christmas and, suffice it to say, this visit was made with shopping in mind. Shops in

Ipswich are densely packed into a relatively small area, so you can get a lot done in the shortest possible time.

The 116 bus back took longer as it ran through a number of villages, even negotiating the far-from-twenty-first-century roadways around Coddenham. Still, it was a pleasant journey back, and I left the bus just as it entered Debenham, to enable me to explore the village more fully. It is an attractive place with a selection of antique shops, pubs and some fine houses. Debenham (pictured here) even has a teapot factory with, of course, a tea-room. There you can see a wide variety of teapots being made, before selecting one to buy.

Expedition 22: Bury St. Edmunds to Ely and back
Bus 11: Bury to Newmarket: 35 minutes
Bus 12: Newmarket to Ely: 35 minutes
To return, the same in reverse was intended, but didn't quite work out

Ely is one of those places that seems as if it's much further away than it actually is. The truth of the matter is, if you are lucky, you can get there from Bury in little over an hour.

I had already discovered that the 11 service between Bury and Newmarket is quick and efficient. Another bonus is that it is intended to link with the 12 service between Ely and Cambridge, so that we were able to step off one bus and onto another that was about to depart. It would have been nice to have been able to see out of the windows but both buses involved in this journey were desperately in need of a good clean.

Ely Cathedral from the tea-room

The journey to Ely takes in Fordham and Soham, but from a distance you are able to spot the towers of Ely Cathedral rising up above the surrounding fens. Just as the soil turns really black, you find you are there.

Ely is a place worthy of spending some time. The Cathedral is the main attraction, both inside and out. Discover the old monastic buildings round the back and have coffee (and cake) in the tea-rooms where, on a fine day, you can enjoy your break with the best view in town.

The riverside area is worth a wander. There are shops of all kinds and a fine local museum. I'd forgotten just how enjoyable a day there can be.

Returning should have been simple, and it began that way. Our bus arrived at Newmarket in plenty of time and we boarded what should have been our last bus to Bury. By Kentford, it became clear all was not well mechanically. Steam or smoke or a combination of the two was issuing from the engine at the rear and whilst we checked where the emergency exits were, the driver contacted base. Another bus was to be sent from Cambridge. The only thing to consider was which would arrive first - the replacement bus or the appointed one scheduled to pass us an hour later.

The replacement duly won the race by five minutes and we found ourselves back at Bury about an hour later than intended, but none the worse for our slight inconvenience.

Dead bus

Expedition 23: Ipswich to Tattingstone, allowing for a walk to Stutton or Holbrook, then returning
Bus 96: To Tattingstone: 10 minutes
Walk to Stutton, then on to Lower Holbrook and Harkstead
Bus 98: Return to Ipswich: 15 minutes

Rather than work from the centre of Ipswich, I chose to park near Bourne Bridge at the end of Wherstead Road as a number of buses stop there including all those I could have chosen to use. Anyone travelling from the centre of Ipswich should add ten minutes to each journey.

This was a pair of short bus journeys with a walk sandwiched between. I left it to the weather to decide how far I would go before returning. As you will see, a number of alternatives present themselves. The bus driver dropped me just where I wanted, approaching Tattingstone village, just the other side of Lemon's Hill Bridge.

Alton Reservoir

Clutching my Ordnance Survey Explorer map 197, I started around Alton Water. This is a well layed out track, wheel-chair friendly and offering spectacular views of the wildlife. You can spot Tufted duck, Great Crested Grebes and a host of other wild-fowl. There are hides halfway round where you can watch in earnest and in peace.

You pass what appears to be a church, but is really the 'Tattingstone Wonder', a folly built by Squire White to enhance the view from his home at Tattingstone Place (see inset picture). Across the Lake, you can see the tower of the Royal Hospital School at Holbrook.

This is an easy and an enjoyable walk, mostly on the level, and there is always something to look at.

Looking towards the Royal
Hospital School and (inset)
the Tattingstone Wonder

Arriving at Stutton, by way of Alton Lane, I ensconced myself in the King's Head, where refreshment was most welcome. Here I was to make my first decision regarding the plan of the day.

I chose to take a different route entirely and to continue walking by footpaths from Stutton to Lower Holbrook, expecting to catch a **98 bus** back.

You begin by following the road past the school and up towards Stutton Church. This is undeniably the best part of the village. You pass several lovely houses, ponds inhabited by herons and fields where I disturbed half a dozen curlew.

What is described as the 'Stour and Orwell Walk' runs along a levee beside the River Stour, and the bird-life is breathtaking. Curlews call and redshanks probe the mud; egrets and sandpipers are all there on view. The Royal Hospital school dominates the landscape on the landward side. All too soon, you are away from the mud-flats and passing reed-beds and heading for the road.

> **Alternative:** You may prefer to head for Upper Holbrook and the Compasses Public House (outside which you can catch a **98 bus** back).

I chose to make for Lower Holbrook, then to continue half a mile up the road to Harkstead, where the Baker's Arms was a treat to behold. All in all, I had walked at least five miles and there was just time to take a little refreshment before my bus (**98**) appeared, bang on time.

Expedition 24: Haverhill to Saffron Walden and back
Bus 59: 42 minutes each way

Two services enable you to make this journey, the 59 and the less well-publicised 18. As a result, you can spend from under an hour to all day in the town of Saffron Walden before making your return. The 59 service takes in a number of interesting villages glorifying in such names as Hellions Bumpstead and Shudy Camps.

You enter Saffron Walden from the top of the Common. I'd advise getting off here. It is only a short walk into town by way of the castle, the museum and one of the finest churches in Essex, so you can make sure you miss nothing. The town itself is a delight, full of old buildings and the sorts of shops that in most towns have given way to international brands. Don't miss the market place (there is a market on Tuesdays & Saturdays), which boasts some of the finest buildings in the town.

There is a downside to all this. It is worth noting that Saffron Walden suffers greatly from traffic.

These pictures give just a hint of Walden's fine buildings

Its ancient streets were never built to take the quantity of cars and lorries that plague it and you have to watch yourself when crossing the road, even well away from the High Street.

Alternative: I visited the town in winter and was enchanted by the place. For two thirds of the year, you can, of course leave exploring the town until later. Instead, stay on the bus and continue on to Audley End, a magnificent eighteenth century mansion in the charge of English Heritage and open to the public from mid-March until mid October.

Saffron Walden market place

This bus trip was another of those where the driver and his customers were clearly regulars on the route; each pick-up and drop was anticipated, and a warm feeling of companionship existed. It seems to me that there is far more going on here than just a means of getting from 'A' to 'B'. The journey is, for many of the participants, a social event; a valuable one at that. The return was pleasant but uneventful. This is a trip I'd certainly like to make again.

Expedition 25: Sudbury to Bures, walk to Nayland and bus back to Sudbury.
Bus 753: Sudbury to Bures: 20 minutes
Bus 84: Nayland to Sudbury: 39 minutes

There are two different routes operating between Sudbury and Colchester. The 753 passes through Bures, Wormingford and West Bergholt, whereas the 84 takes you the other side of the Stour by way of Nayland and Stoke-by-Nayland. Both routes operate hourly in both directions. This is an attractive area, best viewed on foot, so I planned an expedition that included a walk between two of the loveliest villages (just) in Suffolk.

I took a friend with me who is something of an unbeliever where buses are concerned. She needed some convincing that this was a worthwhile means of travel. Things did not start well as we sat close to a youth in possession of a device capable of sending all genuine music-lovers diving for cover. Unfortunately, that isn't really an option when imprisoned upstairs in a double-decker. Luckily, the journey was short and we disembarked beside Bures Church. Another time, this would have proved worthy of a visit, but we were anxious to get started, so after a cursory glance at the river, we headed uphill out of the village.

Beside the river at Bures

70

We took as our reference the O.S. Explorer map 196. You can navigate btween Bures and Nayland in a number of ways. The easiest to follow are the well-marked Stour Valley Path and St. Edmund Way. The Stour Valley Path, as the name suggests, follows lower ground close to the river and passes through Wormingford. We took the St. Edmund Way, and though it was late December, the way was easily walkable without ever becoming too much of a mud-bath.

The first surprise is St. Stephen's Chapel. This restored church lies in the middle of nowhere at the end of a lane. we were fortunate that someone just ahead of us had already been to the Post Office for the key, as inside it proves to be quite remarkable. Several tomb-monuments commemorate the De Vere family, the Earls of Oxford.

St. Stephen's Chapel

Legend has it that this chapel was built on the site of the crowning of King Edmund. True or not, it is a lovely building and proved a pleasant surprise early into our walk.

Much of the route we took was on tracks of one sort or another. Wildlife was plentiful, especially woodpeckers. At one point, the path plunges down past Wissington Grange through woodland and on down to the river to meet the Stour Valley Path which takes you the rest of the way to Nayland. All in all, the walk is about five miles. Pictured below: views along the way

Feeling quite tired, and cooling down rapidly, we were only too pleased to find our bus back to Sudbury arrived bang on time. The return journey takes twice as long as the bus to Bures had. This is not because Sudbury is much farther from Nayland than Bures. It is just that this route doubles back on itself more than once to take in villages like Leavenheath and Assington. Still, you spend an interesting forty minutes passing some of the finest timber-framed buildings in Suffolk. It went some way in convincing my partner that bus travel in Suffolk has much to recommend it.

Expedition 26: Beccles to Lowestoft and beyond
Bus X2: Beccles to Lowestoft: 34 minutes
Bus 1A: Lowestoft to Martham: 1 hour 34 minutes
Bus 1: Martham to Winterton: 11 minutes,
then to Lowestoft: 1 hour 32 minutes

As luck would have it, I chose what was probably the coldest day of the year to travel this, the coldest corner of East Anglia. The occasional pub or coffee-shop would be less a point of indulgence; more a vital warming-room to prepare for the next leg of the journey.

I began at Beccles, though those starting by car may find it easier to park and catch the bus at Gillingham, Worlingham or North Cove.

This journey is unremarkable and has already been mentioned. Lowestoft proved to be bleak and uncomfortable on such a day. The wind drove relentlessly from the East and the wide main shopping street appeared even wider as potential shoppers remained indoors. Beach and piers seemed out of place at such a time.

Winter on Lowestoft beach

This day made use of routes that ran almost every half-hour, six days a week, even in the iciness of January. This meant there should not be too much waiting for buses. Several coffee-shops are close to the bus-station and I had just long enough to warm up before setting off towards Great Yarmouth and beyond.

The road is never far from the sea as you travel through Corton and Hopton, close to Pleasurewood Hills.

Alternative: Burgh Castle is worth a visit. This bus goes no closer than about four miles, but if you change at Gorleston for a number 7 (they run hourly), you will be taken to the old Roman Fort, from whence it is possible to walk back along the River Yare to Yarmouth, a distance of about four miles.

Much of the route passes an endless succession of holiday villages, but there are sights to look out for. Watch out for the remains of St. Margaret's church as you leave Hopton. Approaching Great Yarmouth, you should spot Nelson's Column, only a little smaller than its more famous London cousin. It seems to be in an odd place, and indeed it is - In Victorian times this area was a centre of tourism, but now poor Nelson is buried amongst gas terminals and shabby industrial buildings.

Gorleston is worth a mention. The seaward side of the town is one of the more pleasant parts of this corner of East Anglia. At one point the bus follows the cliff and on a more pleasant day, I'd have happily taken time out right there (see expedition 33).

The bus stops for five minutes in the centre of Great Yarmouth. There is a lot to enjoy here besides the Pleasure Beach. The historic South Quay offers all manner of diversions, especially during the warmer months - the Time and Tide Museum, the river trips, even the town itself are deserving of further attention. Yarmouth's history catches you by surprise - sections of medieval wall and the elegant church of St. Nicholas are there to demonstrate that Yarmouth has more about it than the average seaside resort.

Leaving Yarmouth, you see racecourse and obligatory wind-farm (it is awfully windy here!), and passing through Caister, look out for glimpses of the Roman Fort and Caister Castle.

After that my bus took me past empty holiday centres at Scratby and Hemsby to the village of Martham.

There I discovered that the first pub I found, like much of that part of Norfolk seemed to have shut up shop for the winter. I could hardly blame them. It was bleak.

Martham is not your classically lovely Norfolk village,

but in more clement weather, it is a good starting point for a walk. On consulting the O.S. Explorer Map OL40, you will discover just how close you are to the Broads. With a little imagination, you can devise circular routes that will take you to Horsey, Potter Heigham or round Martham Broad and back along the road to Somerton and the nature reserve, Winterton Dunes.

> **Alternative:** A different return route could involve walking along the River Thurne from Martham Ferrygate Lane or West Somerton Staithe to Potter Heigham or Bastwick, where 736 buses run regularly back to Great Yarmouth. This is a particularly attractive route that takes in a number of Broadland villages.

On this occasion, I headed for warmth and a little comfort. The next bus took me past the Bear at West Somerton and on to Winterton-on-Sea, which on leaving the bus justified its name. Fortunately the Fisherman's Friend Inn served mulled wine and toasted sandwiches and had a fire burning in the hearth.

On a summer's day, I can picture this as an ideal spot. It is a more attractive village than most bordering the North Sea. It has a fine church (and a good web-site describing its history).

I stayed one hour; just long enough to warm the inner man, before catching the next bus back to Lowestoft, and then another to Beccles, where my journey had begun.

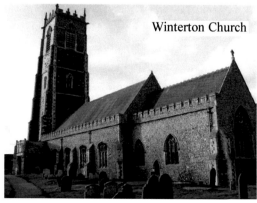

Winterton Church

Expedition 27: Brandon to Norwich, and back to Stowmarket by a devious route

Bus 25A: Brandon to Norwich: 1 hour 22 minutes
Bus 588: Norwich to Bungay: 53 minutes
Bus 580: Bungay to Diss: 40 minutes
Bus 458: Diss to Stowmarket: 63 minutes

Services that only run once a week or less carry a warning. They may arrive in the form of a hire-bus that carries no outward indication that it is the bus you read about in the time-table. Also, they may be early by up to a quarter of an hour in a way that regular service buses are not.

My bus to Norwich, like the one I had taken to King's Lynn from Brandon was a comfortable hire-bus that would have been hard to identify had I not joined a queue of people who clearly knew what to look out for.

Having ambled around Brandon, the bus took a fairly direct route to Norwich, passing around Thetford and through a few villages before sprinting along the A11 to Norwich.

Alternative: One alternative worth noting for a nice Summer's day is the idea of leaving the bus at East Wretham and picking up the Hereward Way (see O.S. Explorer Map 229) which will take you beside the magnificent East Wretham Nature Reserve and through a great deal of Thetford Chase to Santon Downham (a walk of about 6 miles). There, the 200/201 route will take you to Thetford, Brandon or Mildenhall.

It is worth noting that the Bus-Station at Norwich is mainly reserved for Park-and-ride and Norfolk-bound buses (with the exception of Lowestoft buses). Suffolk routes run to and from Ber Street and St. Stephen Street. These are very central and you find you are within easy reach of all that Norwich has to offer.

Norwich Castle

I could write volumes about ways to spend time in Norwich, but that goes far beyond the scope of this book. Suffice it to say, Castle, museums, shops, Cathedral and a host of other attractions await the visitor and it is convenient to remember that Norwich can be reached by a number of Suffolk bus-routes.

Service 5, starting at Southolt and passing through a number of Suffolk places including Bedfield and Eye, operates a twice-monthly service at present. The 588 service links Halesworth and Bungay to Norwich almost hourly six days a week. A half-hourly service (X2) runs between Lowestoft, Beccles and Norwich. Once a week,

Aldeburgh, Leiston and Norwich are connected by the 563. Similarly, the 564 links Wickham Market, Saxmundham and Norwich, and the 569 is a once-weekly service joining Norwich with Framlingham and Stradbroke. All these are in addition to rail and National Express coach services.

I was not returning to Brandon, where I had started, so would not use the same route for my return. Instead, I took the 588 to Bungay, an attractive enough route, passing through Brooke and Hedenham before negotiating the chicken roundabout and on into Bungay, where I was able to hop off one bus and straight onto another heading for Diss. This took a round-the-houses route, but allowed me enough time to enjoy a hot chocolate (with marshmallows floating in it) whilst sitting at the back of Diss Bookshop overlooking the mere with its ducks and gulls.

From there, it was a simple bus journey home to Stowmarket.

Diss Mere

Expedition 28: Bildeston to Cattawade and back
Bus 731: Bildeston to Cattawade: 55 minutes
Bus 92: Cattawade to Ipswich: 41 minutes
Bus 111: Ipswich to Bildeston: 56 minutes

Both Bildeston Market Place and the slip-road at Cattawade serve as useful staging-posts for the bus traveller. As with Martlesham Heath Tesco, a number of bus-routes stop at these points. Also, parking is readily available.

From Bildeston, it is possible to travel via Hadleigh to Manningtree about five times a day. The route is an attractive one, taking you through such villages as Whatfield and East Bergholt.

Alternative: It is possible to leave the bus at East Bergholt and, after viewing the church, walk the narrow lanes that lead to Flatford Mill. Later, you can walk the couple of miles along the Stour (paths run both sides of the river) to Cattawade, or in the opposite direction to Dedham and Stratford St. Mary, where you can catch one of a number of buses back.

On this occasion I stayed on the bus as far as Cattawade. This is not a pretty village; it is a depressing, litter-strewn spot. But it does have the advantage of being close to great bird-watching territory. You hardly need to stray far from the bridge leading across to Manningtree to spot all manner of waders and waterside birds.

A permissive footpath leads you to the Hogmarsh Nature Reserve, complete with hide. In a short time on on a dull January morning, I saw kingfishers, wigeon, dabchicks, redshanks & little-egrets, and many other birds besides.

With the weather deteriorating, I had to cut short my visit. As buses back to Ipswich or Hadleigh are fairly frequent, I was not waiting long. It is worth noting that buses using this slip-road stop both sides of the road. It is not always obvious which side you are meant to be. The 92 takes you to Ipswich by way of Brantham and Holbrook, passing through the grounds of the Royal Hospital School.

My final bus of the expedition was not quite as timetabled. Though clutching the latest copy as reference, I found that the 107 I was looking for was really a 111 and left seven minutes earlier. The bus-driver assured me it had been like this for some time. It made little difference to me other than we passed through Sproughton, Somersham and Offton on our way to Bildeston. However anyone reading the timetable and expecting a bus for Burstall or Elmsett would have been disappointed.

This was an unusual experience - a full bus. We weren't quite reduced to standing room only, but every seat was taken. However, by the time we had cleared Somersham, there were very few of us left.

On arriving back at Bildeston, I experienced what must happen quite often. As the village Market Place is where buses link up with one another, no fewer than four buses were there at the same time to enable passengers to change buses as they made their way between Ipswich, Sudbury, Hadleigh & Stowmarket, and countless small places between.

Expedition 29: From Bury to Diss and back, using two buses and a fold-up bike
Bus 338: Bury to Market Weston: 58 minutes
Then cycle to Wattisfield and Rickinghall (5 miles)
Bus 304: Rickinghall to Bury: 43 minutes

Even though it was late January, I was prepared to give it a try. At best, I am a fair-weather cyclist, but having borrowed a fold-up bike, I was determined to see how it might fit into a bus-trip. I took O.S. Explorer Map 230.

The run from Bury to Market Weston was a delight, passing through attractive places like Ixworth and Bardwell. I counted at least four windmills. The sails were going round on Pakenham Mill.

I could have chosen any one of a number of places to leave the bus. But Market Weston offers a short and relatively safe ride to Wattisfield.

Alternative: A more interesting ride might be to stay on the bus to the next village of Hopton, and then to cycle along the roads that run south of the Little Ouse River, past Knettishall Heath to Euston, before catching the 332 back to Bury.

From where I was dropped, near Market Weston village hall, I found the Thelnetham road. About a mile along the road, a sign points you towards Wattisfield. I only saw one car along the entire three-mile ride.

At Wattisfield, I located the Henry Watson Pottery (pictured here). Open seven days a week, it was an ideal place to take on refreshment (coffee and cake).

I might have caught my bus back from the crossroads nearby, but decided to cycle a further two miles east to the village of Rickinghall. The A143 is not ideal, as there is a section with no allowance made for cyclists. However, after a brisk downhill mile, you find a section of old road that has been designated 'cycle track'. Having reached the brow of the hill, then I found myself freewheeling down to Rickinghall church. It had just started to rain, so I stood in the bus-shelter until my (304) bus appeared to whisk me back to Bury.

Expedition 30: From Sudbury to Castle Hedingham & Halstead and back
Bus 5: Sudbury to Castle Hedingham: 36 minutes
Bus 89: Castle Hedingham to Halstead: 13 minutes
Bus 13: Halstead to Sudbury: 49 minutes
(or Bus 11: Halstead to Sudbury: 37 minutes)

Practically the whole of this journey was spent outside my native county of Suffolk, yet even under the pre-April 2008 rules governing bus-pass use, I was only required to pay for one short journey. The route to Castle

Hedingham is an attractive one, taking you through villages like Gestingthorpe. Hedingham itself is an elegant village with much to attract the casual visitor. There is a fine medieval castle. An internet search for details regarding the castle and the village reveals a number of good sites.

I caught the bus to Halstead from opposite the Bell, as it headed in the opposite direction before turning round at Yeldham and coming back. This would enable a summer visitor to get a lift as far as the steam railway. At weekends from March onwards, the Colne Valley Railway is up and steaming.

Halstead is a typical East Anglian market town. It has a large old water mill known as Townsford Mill that has been turned into a large Antique centre. I amused myself there awhile before catching a bus back to Sudbury. It is worth noting that a (89B) bus-link exists between Haverhill, Halstead and Hedingham.

Expedition 31: From Sweffling to Yoxford and Halesworth and back (via Leiston & Saxmundham)

Bus 118: Sweffling to Saxmundham: 15 minutes
Bus 521: Saxmundham to Leiston: 18 minutes
Bus 196: Leiston to Yoxford: 31 minutes
Bus 521: Yoxford to Halesworth: 18 minutes
Bus 521: Halesworth to Saxmundham: 26 minutes
   (or train: 16 minutes)
Bus 119: Saxmundham to Sweffling: 15 minutes

Why Sweffling? Well, perhaps it was to prove you can plan a circular bus journey from almost anywhere.

I could equally well have chosen Great Glemham. There weren't a lot of passengers along the route from Sweffling to Saxmundham, so I chatted to the driver. It was a most attractive route so the journey passed quickly. I then used the 521 to carry me on to Leiston, getting off at Main Street, by the library, which is where I knew I'd catch my next bus.

The 196 takes you around villages close to the coast. It is a lovely journey, taking you past Leiston Abbey and through Westleton before moving on to Yoxford. The afternoon 196 bus takes in Dunwich, and offers a number of great alternatives to the bus traveller who likes a bit of a walk.

Leiston Abbey with Dunwich Friary above

Alternative: This is terrific route for summer travel. You can leave the bus at Dunwich and walk across Dunwich Heath to Eastbridge (stopping at the Eel's Foot), and on to Leiston Abbey, by way of tracks and footpaths you can find with reference to O.S. Explorer Maps 212 & 231. Return by bus 521.

I arrived at Saxmundham just in time to catch a 521 bus to Halesworth. This is a route I had taken before (see expedition 18) and is one of the few North-South links in our county. However, there is always the East-Suffolk line railway as an alternative means of travel, but remember, you can't use your bus-pass to get a free ride.

Halesworth is a lovely little town that has a lot to recommend it. There is a town trail that is made extra-easy to follow as they've sunk brass discs into the pavement every so often. There's a good collection of independent shops - even a 'tonsorial emporium' known as Sweeney's.

So many of these small towns have fascinating local museums, open during the summer months and staffed largely by volunteers. As well as at Halesworth, I have encountered such museums at Bungay, Clare, Beccles, Harleston, & Saxmundham to mention only a few.

Either bus or train could have taken me back to Saxmundham in time to catch my return bus to Sweffling. On this occasion, I used my bus-pass, and should have caught the next bus back to where I'd started.

Unfortunately, I made for the wrong stop. Probably the safest bet is to catch buses from outside the station. Most seem to go round that way in Saxmundham.

In the end, I had to wait an hour for the next bus. It is worth noting that had I started from Framlingham, I could have taken a 64 to Wickham Market or Woodbridge, then caught a 63 from there to Framlingham.

SAXMUNDHAM

Expedition 32: From Fornham St. Martin to Thetford (with 2 dogs)
Bus 332: Fornham to Thetford: 45 minutes
Bus 84: Thetford to Fornham: 30 minutes

There are books written by people who travelled around all sorts of places with all manner of encumbrances (e.g. Tony Hawkes' 'Round Ireland with a Fridge'), but they had it easy in comparison with my trip taking two excitable dogs to Thetford. It was a fine day and it seemed like a good idea at the time. Fornham St. Martin was a good choice as it is easier to park there than in Bury St, Edmunds and at least three bus routes pass through it.

The journey is probably as attractive as any I've yet encountered in Suffolk. You pass through Breckland-edge villages such as Culford and Ingham, past Ampton Hall and around Livermere, where you catch sight of its two churches - one derelict, the other intact.

Little Livermere church

You see a lot of water, travelling this way - lakes at Ampton and Livermere, Troston and Euston, as well as crossing the Black Bourne several times.

Our time in Thetford was short. The return journey was less impressive than the way we had come. Having toured what seemed to be the least attractive parts of Theford, we travelled quickly back with none of the scenery enjoyed on the way there.

My dogs had competed for attention from me and the other passengers all the way from Fornham. Things were no different on the way back. Both drivers were remarkably tolerant, but I wasn't sorry to return to where I'd started. Still, it is nice to know we have a dog-friendly bus system.

Expedition 33: From Kessingland to Gorleston, then returning to Ipswich, part of the trip by train.
Bus 99: Kessingland to Lowestoft: 29 minutes
Bus 1: Lowestoft to Gorleston Sea Front: 34 minutes
Bus 606: Gorleston Hospital to Oulton Broad:
42 minutes
Train from Oulton Broad South to Melton: 62 mins.
Bus 165: Melton Station to Ipswich: 39 minutes

Knowing a friend was driving to Kessingland gave me the opportunity to start a journey from a different place. I began at the bus shelter opposite Kessingland Wildlife Park. The route I took to Gorleston via Lowestoft involved two routes I'd used before. I knew that service 1 from Lowestoft would take me to the sea front at Gorleston. Though it was January, it was fine and the sun shone on sea and sand, enabling me to imagine just how much nicer this trip would be in July.

Gorleston
pictured
left
& below

The walk from Marine Parade to the James Paget Hospital is under a mile. I chose to make for there as the hospital is on most of the bus routes in that part of Norfolk. The 606 starts there and runs inland as far as Oulton Broad and Carlton Colville. It went right past Oulton Broad railway station, where I knew I needed to catch a train.

I've mentioned before the difficulty in travelling north-south and back by bus in Suffolk. However, the East Suffolk railway line is a handy way of filling that void. True - you can't use your bus-pass, but it is convenient and comfortable and stops at a number of points just in from the Suffolk coast.

I chose to leave the train at Melton station as I knew a 165 bus would pass the door about three minutes later. It was on time and I found myself winging my way back to Ipswich, from where I caught an express bus back to Stowmarket. Five buses and one train - and a bracing walk for good measure.

Expedition 34: From Brandon to Swaffham, then back to Stowmarket by a circular route
Bus 31: Brandon to Swaffham: 1 hour 13 minutes
Bus X1: Swaffham to Gt. Yarmouth: 1 hour 46 min.
Bus 580: Gt. Yarmouth to Diss: 2 hours 1 minute
Bus 456: Diss to Stowmarket: 1 hour 5 minutes

The Saturday bus from Brandon to Swaffham is a bit of a well-kept secret. Operated by Lewis Coaches, it did not appear in the Brandon booklet published by Suffolk County Council that I was referring to. This is a pity as it is a delightful journey that passes through a number of villages and areas of woodland on its ambling way north.

I caught the bus in the High Street after it had run up and down the London Road gathering up its few regular

Swaffham Market

passengers. We headed out on the Mundford Road before leaving main roads behind and plunging into wildest Norfolk. There is much to enjoy - look out for the remains of the old church at Beachamwell and the moated manor house that is Oxburgh Hall (National Trust).

Swaffham is a renowned market town and is well worth a visit on a Saturday at any time of year. I had just time to explore a little and to enjoy the delights of the cafe at the back of the bookshop (more cake!)

This bus service gives you three hours in Swaffham before returning to Brandon. This is what most of the passengers were expecting to do.

Alternative: On the other hand, you could head north to Kings Lynn using service 32, returning later to Brandon on service 40 (as used in expedition 12) . A good plan for a pleasant summer's day would be to take the 32 just as far as Castle Acre, one of England's finest medieval villages. With reference to O.S. Explorer map 236, you can plan a walk that takes you to Narborough Crossroads where buses pass at least twice an hour heading for Swaffham and Norwich. Having read this much of my book, I have no doubt you'll find ways of returning from there.

For my part, the rest of the expedition would be different again. The Xɪ is East Anglia's major super-route, travelling every half-hour from Lowestoft to Peterborough, calling at most major Norfolk towns. I had to try this one, so boarding in Swaffham, I headed for Norwich and beyond. As I was still operating under the pre-April 2008 regulations regarding bus-passes, I asked for a ticket to Lowestoft, though I intended to disembark at Great Yarmouth.

The bus filled up to such an extent that some people waiting at East Dereham were left behind to await the next one. We zoomed into and out of Norwich and  I found myself with a short break in Great Yarmouth.

Alternative: One of the best bus-routes operating in East Anglia is the 736 running from Yarmouth, through Broadland, several times a day to North Walsham. A great day out is to catch this bus from the Market Gates at Yarmouth and travel as far as Hickling. You can follow the Weaver's Way (using O.S. Explorer map OL40), much of it through Nature Reserve, to Potter Heigham where you can catch a returning bus back to Yarmouth.

Seaside towns out of season can be bleak, so I was quite glad to board a 580 heading along the Waveney valley. Much of this route I'd already covered, but the piece between Yarmouth and Beccles was fresh territory. The bus passes Fritton Lake Country Park and St. Olaves before heading across the Haddiscoe Marshes.

Alternatives: With time to spare, you could stop awhile at Fritton or get off at St. Olaves and visit the old priory remains before following footpaths across the marshes and circling round to Haddiscoe village to catch the next bus.
The railway at Haddiscoe, with a station scenically placed beside the Waveney, enables you to catch trains to Norwich, the route passing alongside several of Norfolk's finest Nature Reserves.

I remained aboard my bus as far as Bungay. Knowing it went around the houses here, I leisurely strolled across the churchyard to catch the same bus in St. Mary's Street about ten minutes later.

From there, I was on familiar territory and on arriving at Diss, found my bus back to Stowmarket was already waiting for me. In my travels I have become quite blasé about expecting buses to be punctual. Suffice it to say, once again, they returned me home bang on time.

Expedition 35: From Eye to Framlingham, then back via Saxtead and Diss (Tuesday or Friday only)
Bus 482: Eye to Stradbroke: 23 minutes
Bus 118: Stradbroke to Framlingham: 28 minutes
Walk to Saxtead Mill (about 3 miles)
Bus 100: Saxtead to Harleston: 46 minutes
Bus 580: Harleston to Diss: 23 minutes
Bus 482 (or 114): Diss to Eye: 15 minutes

This journey was added when alterations to expedition 16 removed Eye and Stradbroke from the book. As it happened, this was providential as it turned out to be one of the most enjoyable excursions of the lot.

When you happen upon the small town of Eye, it is worth pausing awhile. Most buses run beside the fine Town Hall and within easy walking distance of the castle and rather lovely church. It was late morning when I began my journey: the antique shops had to be given a miss on this occasion. I needed to catch my bus to Framlingham or it would have meant a further two-hour wait for the next one. I chose the bus-stop just across and down the road from the Town Hall. The 482 now terminates at Stradbroke, but is timed to link with the 118, which appeared just eight minutes after the first bus had left.

From there, it was a splendid run via Laxfield and Dennington, entering Framlingham around lunchtime. This was one of several of my expeditions that has included a walk - this time following a bridle-path marked on the map (O.S. Explorer map 212) as 'Earl Soham Lane.'

This leads you from the top of Brook Lane in a westerly direction until you can see Saxtead Mill, when the track turns north towards the mill. The final part of the path deviates around houses and gardens, finally bringing you to the road close to the Old Mill House Inn.

Here I was able to enjoy a pint and light bite before ambling across the green towards the Mill. This is well worth a visit, but I had not allowed time on this occasion.

I thought I had more time than I had. But as I'd discovered previously, occasional buses like the 100 service that run only on a Tuesday and Friday have a habit of turning up early. I'd bought an ice-cream from a van on the green. There was barely time to consume it as I chased to flag down my bus. To be fair, occasional buses are provided to take villagers to town once a week. Drivers are not used to picking up extra passengers in between.

Still, it was a pleasant rural ramble that carried me to Harleston. From there, I arrived at Diss having just missed a 114 bus, but just in time to return to Eye (pictured here) on a 482.

 Travelling the length and breadth of the county of Suffolk and beyond has enabled me to enjoy town and country-side in a whole new way.

And remember, this was wintertime. With these jouneys behind me and the prospect of summer and a more versatile bus-pass in my pocket, I now expect to put it to even better use. Using my bus-pass in the warmer, lighter times and with fewer limits as to how far I might travel will be an entirely different experience.

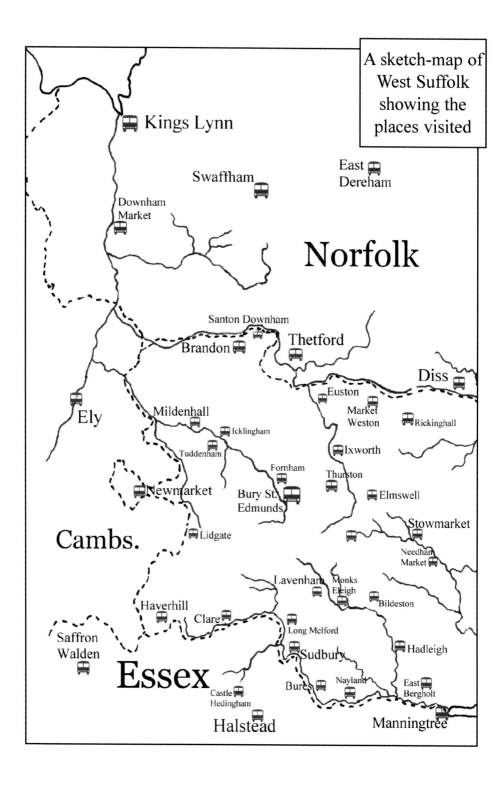

A sketch-map of West Suffolk showing the places visited

Kings Lynn

East Dereham

Swaffham

Downham Market

Norfolk

Santon Downham

Brandon

Thetford

Diss

Euston

Ely

Mildenhall

Icklingham

Market Weston

Rickinghall

Tuddenham

Ixworth

Fornham

Thurston

Newmarket

Bury St. Edmunds

Elmswell

Cambs.

Lidgate

Stowmarket

Needham Market

Lavenham

Monks Eleigh

Bildeston

Haverhill

Clare

Long Melford

Saffron Walden

Hadleigh

Sudbury

Essex

Bures

Nayland

East Bergholt

Castle Hedingham

Halstead

Manningtree

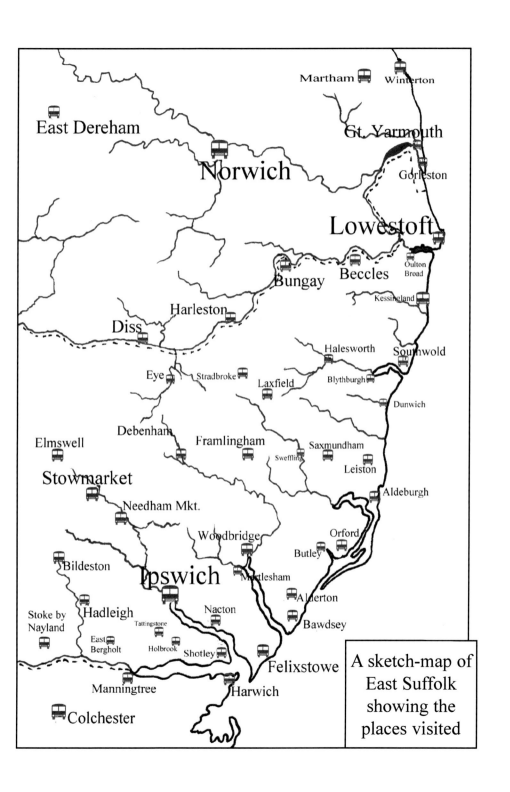

A sketch-map of East Suffolk showing the places visited